Sengupta did not write the three books to come up with a trilogy. He had rather gathered his observations — of 'self' and the world around him ... like all conscious writers of all times! The three books, *My Glass of Wine*, *The Reverse Tree*, and *Healing Waters Floating Lamps*, collectively form a trilogy — a souvenir that we have curated with care. We wish to connect with the global readers through history and time.

 hawakal creative

DREAMS OF THE SACRED
AND
EPHEMERAL

KIRITI SENGUPTA

HAWAKAL PUBLISHERS

Published by **Hawakal Publishers**, 185, Kali Temple Road,
Nimta, Calcutta 700049, India

Website: www.hawakal.com

Contact: info@hawakal.com

First edition [India]: April 2017

ISBN-13: 97893-85782-62-6 [Hardbound] India Edition
ISBN-13: 97893-85782-63-3 [Paperback] USA Edition

Cover photograph credit: Plabon Das
Cover design: Bitan Chakraborty

Photography Credit (for *Healing Waters Floating Lamps*):
Arindam Chowdhury and Somnath Chatterjee

Price: INR 350 / USD 15

Critical Acclaim for Kiriti Sengupta

Sengupta's short poems mirror the Japanese Haikus, grasping the mystery and miracle of life in a cryptic idiom.

The Hindu Literary Review

These poems are different from the run-of-the-mill Indian English poems in being far closer to our humdrum daily experiences and their baffling paradoxes and cruel ironies.

K. Satchidanandan

The way [Sengupta] has purposefully retained ordinariness in his language [in *My Glass of Wine*] is a show of humility with innate sense and respect for the aesthetics.

Linda Ashok

Kiriti Sengupta's [*My Glass of Wine*] is a bricolage that reveals as much as it hides; like the poet, the reader too becomes a bricoleur who responds to the myriad hues of the creation in his unique way. The reader and the poet coalesce; the poet's intuition merges with the reader's perception.

Muse India

Sengupta writes in an original voice and his poems capture mosaic and rhymes with truth. A natural writer with a sharp and sympathetic mind, [he] has woven his personal anecdotes with aplomb.

Gopal Lahiri

Sengupta is a masterful narrator in prose and verse through a genre of literature that I may call, 'soul script.'

Seshu Chamarty

The strength of [*The Reverse Tree*] lies in what could have been for many blocks of weakness or shortcoming: its uncanny precision, its unmistakable casualness in tone intermixed with occasional gravity of the subject matter, and most importantly its immaculate simplicity of narration coupled with enticing poeticism in its language. What is contained inside this slimmest structure is a mine of dynamite: all it needs is a spark in the form of concentration and a bit meditation and mediation, and what it gives, besides many things, is a spark in the form of self-realization.

Indian Journal of Comparative Literature and Translation Studies

In *Healing Waters Floating Lamps*, Sengupta's poetry refuses to be limited, addressing everything from meditation practice to achieve spiritual perfection, Hindu rituals involving the Ganges River, the precarious position of a bride when the family into which she married is hostile, photography, and classical poetry. Most poems make use of very forthright, unpretentious language and appear to express simple observations from the poet's life. Other poems are lyrical, such as "the mother [bird] changes to sky," a line that makes a reader's heart leap up with both delight and recognition.

Donna J Snyder

Kiriti Sengupta's poems are at once lonely, spiritual and a mystique of the open wide world punctuated with existential questions. Throughout the poems there are reverberations of the infinite pinned down by a finite well-ordered reality. But the subversive elements dominate the poems — this well ordered reality should be transcended into the metaphysics of life. Sengupta's poems are no ontology; they are direct references to life, the rustic world and sometimes to relationships. They may be direct statements, but their innards are complex and philosophical.

The Shillong Times

Spirituality flows like ebb and flow of the tide through these short, staccato verses, like water in the womb, in eyes, in rivers, and in oceans. You find transcendence in unlikely places such as in the eyes of a mother bird and in a fish tank, and questions in places where you expect answers, such as in the yearnings of aged parents, in a river that bears Gods, in birth, in love, and in worship. And in this sense the lyrical title *Healing Waters Floating Lamps* mimics the overarching spiritual philosophy of the book, which is fluid like water and the verses that are like fireflies, each illuminating a separate, unique patch of darkness for a fraction of a second.

Red Fez

A pioneering genius in poeticizing yogic science, [Sengupta] emerges as a rare poet. Through yogic poetry, he has dared to tread the inexplicable labyrinthine path of literature that only the literate few would dare do.

Contemporary Vibes

Contents

Foreword   i

Alap   vii

My Glass of Wine

As I Traversed	5
My Glass of Wine	10
My Sister's *Bhaiya*	15
Southern Affiliation	20
Rains	28
Clips	35
My Master and the Cover	41

The Reverse Tree

Anti-Clock	59
In Others' Shoes	61
Long … A Metaphor	65
Crisis	69
Jet Lag	83
Reversal … Reverse All	88

Healing Waters Floating Lamps

Beyond The Eyes	111
After Bath	113

Evening Varanasi	115
River Of Tears	117
Unravel	119
Initiation	121
In Dusty Feet	123
Eyes Of A Yogi	125
Communion	127
The Enlightened Master	129
Color Code	131
Clarity	133
Indian Matrimony	134
Namesake	136
Mellifluous Cry	139
Secure A River	141
Memorandum of Understanding	143
Sleep ... Yet To Arrive	145
Celluloid	147
Fish-Lip	149
Scratches Are Only Human	151
The Odd Number	153
The Sun	155
Close Circuit	156
The Morgue	157
Give Me More Of Life	159
Adios	161
Since Time Unknown	163
Notes	165-168
Acknowledgements	169-170

Foreword

I read Kiriti Sengupta's trilogy *My Glass of Wine,*
The Reverse Tree and *Healing Waters Floating Lamps*
in the order in which, I think, they were written
and the order in which I have listed them. To
read them in sequence is a journey, whether your
own or the author's may be inconsequential. The
journey is one that draws the reader further and
further into personal reflection — but reflection
from the world around us into the inner self.
Worldly observations become the occasion for
explorations of meanings: of the self and its
status within the world and within
consciousness, and of life's journey from birth
to death.

Both *My Glass of Wine* and *The Reverse Tree* contain more prose than poetry. The first volume is almost innocently self-exploratory and revelatory: the poet's first encounter with literature [in the context of his first date with his future wife], his family, his sister, his son, his city of origin. He explores his own religion and is introduced to Christianity, an introduction, which he, as a young man, attempts to make the most of, but disappointingly so. Each topic provokes a poem to capture its essence. We see not only the relationship of poetry to that which is meaningful in the poet's life, but the evolution of his ability to express these meanings in poetic lines. *The Reverse Tree* explores even deeper roots of personality and experience. Momentary but memorable encounters with friends [as in "In Others' Shoes"] teach the poet a lesson, which he generalizes to become a lesson for all of us about life. In "Long ... a Metaphor" he explores the role of long hair in the poet's definition of his identity ... and touches upon the multiple sexual identities that inhabit each of us and become the core of his long essay "Crisis." This beautiful uninhibited exploration of sexual orientation and its relationship to one's humanity moves from an examination of the poet Sumita Nandy and her work, to India's bias and discrimination against homosexuality to a personal narrative of an encounter with someone who is transgender. This latter episode is a model of valuing the worth of the individual and not being distracted by his or her sexual orientation, despite that being such a large factor in the person's identity.

Finally, in *Healing Water Waters, Floating Lamps* the author becomes a full-fledged poet, abandoning, for this volume, the use of prose to express his meanings and relying completely on poetry. The results are stunningly beautiful. The themes that were initiated in the earlier works are here [as are some of the poems], as is Sengupta's close observations of the world around him. Again, we see the power of the real world to provoke the deepest of inner meditations. The first four poems all focus upon water: the river Ganges and its power to cleanse the soul and tears flowing from the eyes in rivers, being reminded that "*Not all rivers succeed to unite.*"

Stone statues and their making provide a window into the spirit. And my favorite, about the yearning [and futility] of becoming more [or different] than you are, and the sense of humor to accept it, is a poem titled "In Dusty Feet."

I was about to prostrate,
But refrained from paying an obeisance
To the enlightened Master
His great toes housed
Some holy grains of dust
He took good care of his feet, I guessed,
And I picked the grains as quickly
As to place them on my head

I followed his footsteps,
Even on the dusty roads
I wished to become such pious grains
So as to stay attached with his feet forever

I turned back as I failed,
And could not hold the grains either
On my big toes…

God remained thumb-sized with dusty feet.

While Sengupta's poems touch the spirit, and often deal with spiritual matters, they are uniformly grounded in the world around us. No better example is his poem, "Scratches are Only Human" and its memorable lines:

Few beautiful scratches, deep within,
Soft marks, palpable even after months—
No wounds, but tiny scratches brown
Soothing, mesmerizing in between

Kiriti Sengupta's three books are not just a journey, but a commentary on how to use poetry to express that which is inexpressible otherwise, even in prose. They accomplish this task very well.

Casey Dorman
Editor, *Lost Coast Review* [California]

Alap

What good does an introduction do in a collection of creative writing? Does it serve any purpose? Does it benefit a book at all? These were the questions I nurtured when *The Unheard I*, my first book written in English, was released back in 2013. I'm aware of the fact that most readers tend to avoid the introductory segments, which consist of a foreword by a guest author and an introduction or a preface from the author of the collection. The question remains: Why on earth does an author write an introduction to a book?

I believe an introduction plays a pivotal role in establishing a good rapport with the readers. When I say "rapport" I mean "bonding;" I mean a "connection." An introduction sounds funny when, at an awards function, the presenter says, "The recipient of the award needs no introduction," and introduces the winner formally to the audience. Would you call it sarcastic or self-contradictory?

A harmonious relationship between two people in India starts with a formal *alap*. When I say *alap* it reminds me of the critically acclaimed *Alaap*, a Hrishikesh Mukherjee movie which got two stalwart Indian actors performing together for the first time: Amitabh Bachchan and Rekha. Both *alap* and *alaap* are pronounced as *aalaap*, and it means a prologue to an Indian classical performance. You may refer to it as an improvisation, but honestly *alap* is no longer an improvised opening section delivered without any preparation.

The book in hand, *Dreams of the Sacred and Ephemeral*, is one cohesive collection of the three books I have authored: *My Glass of Wine*, *The Reverse Tree*, and *Healing Waters Floating Lamps*. I had different objectives as I wrote them and, trust me, I had no intention, even in the wildest of my dreams, to come up with a poetic trilogy. My reviewers marked them as a trilogy and, finally, it was *Hawakal*, the publisher, who persuaded me to publish this collection. I'm happy today as I write the introduction; but then, I'm sad as well as I miss Don Martin, one of my dearest friends in the United States and editor of all the three books, who has perhaps been advised by his doctor to stay away from the computers. An ambiguous, mixed reaction, I can tell you!

When I looked upon the Preface and Introduction of the first edition of *My Glass of Wine* they read lengthy and monotonous. A few lines appeared out of focus as well. Unlike some serious writers I have no objection to being "popular," for popularity has nothing to do with pieces that are categorized as "literary," or oppositely, "chick-lit." There is no fight between the class and the mass, and one must remember a "class" essentially belongs to the "mass."

In the first edition of *My Glass of Wine* I wrote:

In recent times we are commonly referred to as "Indian English" writers or poets. Honestly speaking I don't completely concur with this title, and I would like to be known only as an Indian author. In spite of being a developing country, English is no longer a foreign language in India. English is treated as an international language, and is predominantly used in all formal affairs. Moreover, we have here many authors who are regularly writing in English. I don't really know if someone is trying to remind us of our native tongues! Writing in English is no sin, nor is it a lesser offense. This is just a matter of personal choice.

What I forgot to write was I would love to be marked as a Bengali English author. I'm a born Bengali, and if my writing does not ooze the essence of Bengali culture and traditions I'm only ignoring my being on the earth. Worldwide, Bengalis share a few common interests: spirituality, customs and cuisines, affinity towards *Rabindrasangeet* [songs by Tagore], and sports and politics, among others. Now being a Bengali these will invariably influence my writing, especially the flavor.

Madhu, a friend and fellow poet, has been introduced in his debut book of poems, *Make Me Some Love to Eat*, as: "A Tanjore-Maharashtrian with a Bengali *bhadralok* sensibility, blame it on his upbringing in Kolkata..." One of his poems, "Mudded," bears words like *khejur gur*, *alta* and *gamcha*, which are not only Bengali, they rather bring flashes from the Bengali tradition and culture.

As far as stylistics is concerned I had commented on it in the first edition of *My Glass of Wine*:

> As a journalist-author I have often asked poets and writers if they were influenced by some other authors. Most of the time they have named some eminent poets or novelists or some landmark books that influenced their writing style. If I were to name some, I would have said: 1. Shabana Azmi, the distinguished artiste of Indian cinema and theatre, and 2. Suhel Seth, the

quintessential agony-uncle from Calcutta. Shabana transformed me with her speech that was once aired on our national television channel, *Doordarshan*. She had been asked to share the secret of her speaking fluent English. She said, "If you want to speak in English, you need to think in English first." This was extremely mind-hitting, for the average Indian usually translates their words into English as they speak or write. "Thinking in English" is indeed a unique process that enables one to gather the finer nuances of the language, however difficult. On the other hand, Suhel impressed me with his unique take on different queries that his readers posed. He actually speaks his mind, and is perhaps not bothered about the effects his response imparts.

I can remember one of the first few readers of *My Glass of Wine* was seriously annoyed to read the name of Suhel Seth as my inspiration. He thought no "great literature" could ever be created if the author got inspired by someone who was identified as a sex-counselor. He was even more disappointed as the book was labeled a bestselling title at a prominent Indian e-commerce portal within a few weeks from its first release back in 2013. I think the counselors not only suggest ways for betterment, they do work on their speech [words] to influence their clients. A counselor is no lesser than a poet or novelist, nor are their clients lesser than their readers. One must realize writers don't write bestsellers; readers make a book popular. If a writer exhibits some control or understanding of the readers' minds, blame those who have remained apathetic towards the buyers.

Both *My Glass of Wine* and *The Reverse Tree* have been praised and reviewed in India and abroad. But, the reviewers have never failed to express their amazement while commenting on the "genre" of the book. I wondered how important it was to categorize a book!

When you say, "This is non-fiction," I'm sure you won't have many readers. If you say, "Hey! This is poetry," I believe, you will appeal even to fewer readers. I can say: *"My Glass of Wine,* and *The Reverse Tree* are two books written in the English-language, and in several ways." I think by categorizing a book we only confuse the potential readers.

Presently editors and critics prefer non-abstract poetry. A few of them like to read nature poetry. My point is: Poetry deserves to have more than one layer of meaning. If we remove metaphors, poetry loses its charm. If we remove the philosophical content, poetry turns disastrously mundane irrespective of how one arranges and breaks the lines. You may read a short verse here:

The Source

For years I've been searching
the flavors of
birth and death

Do they exude the same?

Aren't they as fragrant and fresh
as the ancient fruit?

Here is another free verse:

I let you go, for I love you
The rainbow has disappeared a long time ago
The horizon looks clean and sunny
as the rain dropped in seven hues

In those drops of color I remained
I remain even now
I…
And you were the drop-filled windy cloud

I can remember, I sent it to a well-known editor and publisher of an acclaimed American journal that offered a critique of my poem. The publisher wrote: "Love poems are hard to pull off and I don't think this does so." I failed to understand why and how did the publisher mark it a "love poem?" On the contrary, I think the lines create an aura of "interior monologue," written in verse, which is not necessarily a love poem. Even if I agree with the publisher, isn't "love" a universal, humane chemistry that is prevalent across the nations? Can you possibly consider love cliché? They say, modern poetry must avoid cliché and obvious things. Love, among other emotions, is perhaps missing from the theme and syntax of new-age poetry, thus, keeping readers at bay!

Salability should not affect the quality of poetry. Even if you follow Eliot can you ensure a good market? If no, why would you not write something personal? My feelings and experiences may not be exclusive or unique, and I'm sure many people can readily connect with my life and living. In *My Glass of Wine*, and *The Reverse Tree* I intended to offer shreds of autobiographic images along with some poetry weaved into the prose. I think, poetry should not read too abstract! It can be made accessible and enjoyable as well. Unless we work on it, poetry can never reach its pinnacle again. Gone are the days when poetry was targeted to its exclusive readers. Considering the pathetic decrease in its readership all over the world, shouldn't the poets come forward with interesting packages? Some readable works, which will be enjoyed by a large number of booklovers?

Be a bit cautious, dear readers, you won't find a smooth transition from one chapter to another, especially in *The Reverse Tree*. My life has never sailed smoothly, and whenever I raised a complaint, my Enlightened Master opined, "If there is a storm in your life, be assured, you are on the right path." I believe, when lives can be random, why would I possibly plan to order and smoothen the transitions? Let them remain as-it-is ... I will let you probe the real author!

I can remember, during an informal meeting with one of my reviewers, Gopal Lahiri, an earth scientist and a prominent Indian poet [who writes in English], he urged, "You have included so many poems in *My Glass Of Wine*, and *The Reverse Tree*, it is high time you think about an exclusive collection of your poems." This was, in fact, the source of inspiration of the making of *Healing Waters Floating Lamps*.

I consider poetry my existence. It is indeed challenging to successfully present philosophical poems to a larger audience. I strongly believe without readers an author is absolutely null and void. Now that *Hawakal*, the publisher, is publishing the three books together, I'll rather ask my readers: "Did I live up to Baudelaire's quote, 'Always be a poet, even in prose?'"

Kiriti Sengupta
March 21, 2017
Calcutta

The Three Books

My Glass of Wine, The Reverse Tree, and *Healing Waters Floating Lamps.*

My Glass of Wine

*It was not only the wine, but
that the glass was mine*

"Now that she had nothing to lose, she was free"

Paulo Coelho

To

hülya yilmaz, Ph.D.

As I Traversed

Would I name it an encounter? Well, my first encounter with Bengali literature started way back in the year 1995 at the famous Coffee House of Calcutta. I must put it in place that I remain a lazy reader even now. Those were my golden times of youth and vigor. And it was my first date with my girlfriend, Bhaswati, whom I married after six years of courtship. As we sat on the chairs and ordered two cups of coffee, I initiated a "not-so-romantic" conversation with her. I considered my first date boring as I was asked, "Did you read *Shesher Kobita* [*The Last Poem*] by Tagore?" I went speechless, and waited for a while. I was trying to organize my response. Until then I never had heard of something like

Shesher Kobita. I politely replied, "Look, I don't read poetry at all." Bhaswati flashed a quick smile, and I was relieved. Of late I realized that Bhaswati had considered my response in a light spirit! Dear readers, hopefully you are aware that *Shesher Kobita* is a landmark novel by Tagore.

I made my mind to read the novel as fast as it was possible. In those days we used to mark our love letters with literary quotations. Letter writing remains a lost art, and trust me, I loved writing pretty long letters in spite of my poor Bengali vocabulary! This is indeed a pity, and I do repent on my inability to master the world's sweetest language, which is Bengali. But, reading a novel for the sake of my girlfriend was not my cup of tea at all. In the meantime Bhaswati informed me that I could well buy a cassette of an audio play of *Shesher Kobita*, for she thought that I might have been occupied with my text books of Dental Surgery.

Oh, poor she! Being a student of North Bengal University I used to live in Siliguri, which is a prominent town in the district of Darjeeling. Our college hostel was quite distant from the

6

main town, and I had to travel for almost an hour to fetch a cassette of the audio play. The intra-city conveyance was not so prompt then. However, as I switched on my Philips Walkman I was taken aback! A play enacted through voice renditions by noted Bengali artistes from Calcutta. It was touching, enchanting, mesmerizing, and soul stirring, to say the least. A moody composition by Tagore...

Thus began my journey into the world of literature. As I said before, I remain a lazy reader even now. I do not prefer reading long writings, be it poetry or prose. And I believe that there are numerous others who belong to my category of readers. My observation is such: Writers are indifferent at times, and they think that their writings will be chosen by many who may do justice to their efforts invested in the literary endeavors. As a reader I have tried to find a clue. Honestly speaking, I have failed to derive anything satisfactory.

Literature plays varied roles in human lives; the first and the foremost role is entertainment! What about poetry? Do poems entertain the readers? Poetry may prove to be captivating, enchanting, melodious, rhythmic and fantasizing, but it can never entertain in the first place. Poetry delivers. Poetry communicates. Poetry bridges up. Poetry inspires. Poetry evokes. Poetry provokes. Poetry enlightens. Poetry illumines. Poetry heals. And through all these facets poetry may entertain its readers finally! My new attachment to the world of Bengali poetry set out with the poem, *Tui* [Thee]. It had been dedicated to one of my disciple brothers, who through his deeds left behind an ill-defined, seemingly endless agony, which acted as the "initiator" within me, the poet Kiriti. I have been fortunate to have met with a few of the serious Bengali writers and poets, who have motivated me enough to carry on with my dream of being the author of literary endeavors. Writing, I think, is all about consumption — the more you consume the fuel of your being, the better the outcome!

Consumption

Consumed time
like an infant consuming
milk; inevitable
it remains.

Killed essence of
the eternal soul; and consumed,
essentially I remain...

My Glass of Wine

I was studying Dentistry, and was in my final year of studies. I was introduced to the local church by one of my college friends. It was under the auspices of the Church of North India [C.N.I.]. She was eager to get me baptized at the earliest, as she found me her soul-mate. To be honest, this particular notion of being a soul-mate was something weird! And I never nurtured such a belief myself. However, visiting the church, and getting involved with the weekly sessions of *Bible* reading fascinated me. I was quick to gather the nuances of Christianity. It deserves a mention that the lady-friend who took me to the church was herself a Hindu, and belonged to an orthodox Brahmin family. It was seemingly paradoxical! My family was not so strict about me changing the way of my lifestyle. Yet I didn't have the courage to convey the news to my father, who was particular about certain regulations of the so-called Hinduism. He was an initiated devotee of Belur Mutt, a prominent organization founded by Swami Vivekananda, a foremost follower of Paramhansa Sri Ramakrishna. We used to have some ritual-based religious acts at home at frequent intervals. Nevertheless, I continued with dentistry and regular readings of *The Bible*. What was so inspiring about Christianity? Well, I found its prayer sessions interesting indeed. The way a group of people prays towards the fulfilment of a certain goal is, in fact, the most fascinating quality of the Christians. I remember, when I approached the Father [of the said church] about my older sister being unwell of her marital life, he stood upright and advised all the followers to pray for my sister. They prayed aloud. It was mindboggling! Trust me, it gave an immediate relief, and my older sister was able to find some peace in her life! One morning I went to the church and told Father, "I wish a formal baptism." The Father said, "You need to get spiritually baptized first." As I inquired about the way of getting baptized spiritually, he said, "Invite Jesus into your life. Invite Him wholeheartedly. You will find changes on your own as He comes into your heart." I was desperate. I closed my eyes and with full concentration and I urged, "Oh Jesus! I am inviting you to come in, and be my savior." I fail to remember what happened next. All I can remember now is this: I felt some unique sensation within, there was a mild headache, and I had interestingly tender eyes. As soon as I looked at Father he said, "You are done, my boy!" It came as a big surprise. These were, in fact, a few initial words I wanted to share with you all, for my first sip of red wine has had its relation with my being a part of Christianity. I vividly remember I was first offered homemade red wine in a Christian congregation. Until then I never tasted any kind of alcoholic beverage. I was told that red wine makes one remember the divine blood that Jesus sacrificed! Frankly speaking, I never questioned the logic in favor of or against such a statement until I experienced the so-called Hindu Tantric way of worshipping God!

For those who are unaware of *Tantra* I would like to convey that alcoholic beverage is used in sufficient quantity during the conventional Tantric rituals. Here the priests prefer to sport blood red attires. They consider the color symbolic of the divine power. On the other hand, the word *Qurbani* is a familiar term with the Islamic people. Irrespective of its true implication you will find sacrifices of living animals [goats and cows] in their traditional festivals. The sheer sight of blood and the deafening screams of the species are perhaps linked with prosperity, energy, and vigor. Now if I correlate these things together, I find the elements of blood, power, alcohol, and red associated intimately with divinity. I won't mind if you find me controversial, but I should raise the question: How can the amorphous God be related to any worldly element? Is it essential to associating with blood?

Blood Related

It was not branded, but a homemade wine.
Intimately divine,
I drank it first
right after I was spiritually baptized.
Ah! My olden golden days of north India.
I often wondered
why the wine was made and offered!

I had been corrupt...

The Hindu Tantrics prefer the sight
of red light.
Be it of the attire, or
the holy sacrifice!

And in conventional practice of Islam
Qurbani is made a popular station.

You and I
the Father and son
the legacy goes on
inevitable — impeccable,
blood relation…

My Sister's *Bhaiya*

I'm some four years younger than my sister. Yet she calls me *Bhaiya* [that means older brother in Hindi]. In my native tongue [Bengali] *Bhaiya* and *Bhai* are almost synonymous, and they mark the younger brother. I don't know, and have not yet asked my sister the reason behind naming me such. As a kid I was the only one who sported this name in my neighborhood. Trust me, although I was not a famous kid, *Bhaiya* was. In recent times I have noticed that this name is being frequently used in Bengali communities as well. Naturally, *Bhaiya* has lost its charm. In India names bear meanings, and have their own charm that we generally associate with the

15

persons concerned. Surprisingly I have not seen a single Christian with the name "Jesus" in India! But amongst the so-called Hindus, you will have plenty of *Shiv*, *Krishna*, *Vishnu*, *Narayana*, *Ganesh*, *Durga*, *Lakshmi*, *Saraswati*, etc. They are all the gods, and goddesses. Religion has left its profound mark in the psyche of the Indians, but has failed to alter their behavioral pattern. Thankfully I was named [Kiriti] after an important character of *The Mahabharata*. And he was no god.

Please, allow me to work on the word "name." If I replace the initial consonant 'n' with yet another, 'f', we get "fame." Now, what is fame without a name? Again, what will you possibly do with your name if you aren't famous? Sounds tricky, does it? I often replace the 'n' with a 'g', and find it "game." Remembering an old Bengali song that bore an English line: *It's a game, it's a game, it's a game…* Well, all is not game when it comes to the name. Elderly Indians often name the newborns after the names of the gods and goddesses, for whenever they call the kids by their names the divine names are uttered, and

16

chanted effortlessly! Nevertheless, I am much pleased to deliver my poetic thesis on "name," and I am sure you will love it.

Namesake

1.

Whispers the tale of your character,
color and its fragrance merge to call it
a Rose.
A lot matters,
if you remember
the name...

2.

With sheer innocence told the boy
the story of his watching movies
in a hall named *Nadia Talkies*.
Sharing the same story for many a times,
uttered the name, talkies, and had his face
shine!
Humble was the hall,
so were its viewers. Alas!
It is no more, and got abolished
by the estate promoters!
The boy is now a grown up man

Nadia remains in its reel-can.

3.

The womb carries water — so do your eyes,
water builds the fetus
that becomes I...

It's a room for your eyes;
under the name—
"Rely"

4.

Significant indeed — carrying yourself
"Crucify" is Christ-filled
I remember, and my mind turns candle-lit

They pinned it before, will do that now and
again...
No arrangements of incenses though!

God & Life;
moving apart...

Here ends my thesis "Namesake." I'm no
Shakespeare to say, "What is in a name?" A
name is expected to be the gateway of the

personality, and individuality. In India as we offer our homage to our seniors, they bless us saying, "May you brighten the names of your parents." I remain *Bhaiya* to my older sister until now, and she hates to consider my age, which is no lesser than thirty-eight! According to Tagore the beauty of humans cannot be entirely perceived only through our sensory organs, and a name aids in the process of beautifying through imagination. Dear readers, let us be name-filled. Let the world realize that we actually hold our names.

Southern Affiliation

Apart from New Delhi, which is my maternal home, the only place I have frequented until now is Madras, otherwise known as Chennai. It was in the year 1998 I went there first accompanying my senior colleague, Dr. Falguni Maji. We participated in a workshop, conducted by the Independent Medical Practitioners Association of India [I.M.P.A.I.], Madras. It was a five-day conference and we were finally awarded the title: *Fellow of the College of Independent Practitioners* [F.C.I.P.]. We were first exposed to the concept of professionalism in the said conference that housed some eminent professional medical practitioners from Madras. We were taught three important aspects of independent practice: 1.

Never underestimate your patients, and don't judge them by their physical appearances; 2. Doctors are not god-men; they are similar to other professionals like the engineers, lawyers, architects, etc.; 3. Keeping abreast with newer developments through regular study of journals, websites, etc. We had a renowned Orthodontist as the speaker, who lectured about the implications of Arjuna's *Visvarup Darshan* as depicted in *The Mahabharata*! This is for those who aren't familiar with the epic: In *The Mahabharata* Lord Krishna allowed Arjuna to envision the whole of the world within His mouth. Our revered speaker wonderfully explained the oral manifestations of systemic diseases in the light of literature! Thus, Madras became one of my favorite southern destinations, and honestly speaking, as an author of some literary enterprises I have corroborated the teachings that I learnt in my writing. The city exudes joy, excitement, culture, traditional values, professional excellences, and much more! Moreover, Madras serves the world's softest *Idli*s [steamed cake made of ground rice and lentils] that are mouthwatering and delicious. Let me share a poem which I wrote keeping in mind the joy I gathered from visiting the city, Madras.

The Encyclopedia

I have not reached yet
the science of you; I know
I am glued to, and stand still
with some fixation.

Since period unknown
you spin, and continue to swivel;
you have a firm grip.

Faulty are my limbs,
they tilt even on the steady floor;
I readily realize
it is all in my mind
as the sky swings.

You spin, and continue to swivel
since period unknown…

Next in my list is Udupi, one of the prominent temple towns of southern India. I had been there twice, and I am eagerly looking forward to visiting the place again in the near future. Udupi has its unique charm, and hosts innumerable temples all along its length and breadth! I remember that we used to wake up right at 4am listening to the holy chants that echoed around the air. Ah! It was an absolute bliss. In Udupi I was first served tea in a small stainless steel cup. I found their tea-service truly unique. They prepared tea, usually with milk, and poured it into a small steel cup. Next they took a shallow steel bowl to cover the cup. Now holding the entire unit firmly in hand they reversed it upside down. Tea was served only this way, and you need to carefully reverse the direction of the cup again as you are ready for the sip. Although the whole mechanism sounds interesting, it is cumbersome for the first time visitors and tourists. But the advantage of this process lies in the fact that the tea remains warm until you take the first sip. Keeping warmth is perhaps the mantra of south-Indian people. Bengalis were once known for their hospitality worldwide, but it is indeed with the southern public you will be able to taste the true flavor of the Indian culture, which boasts *Atithi Devo Bhava* [Guest is God]. Below is a free verse that is a memoir of my Udupi visit.

Market

World, Peace, and Poetry:
they walk with associating hands
And God prevails
with all pros and cons—
He is dated, yet in!

Look at your seniors,
all those wise people;
they spread love, and
receive God.
They hate the sin...

My southern affiliation won't end if I don't mention a personality from southern India. He is the one who inspired, and encouraged me in my literary endeavors. He was the first reviewer of my maiden English-language nonfiction, *The Unheard I.* Let me share a few words on Mr. Atreya Sarma Uppaluri. He is a retired executive of the State Bank of India, and lives in Hyderabad. A literary worker, Atreya is a well-known translator, poet, and a writer, who has been working as a core editor of *Muse India*, one of the reputed online literary journals published in India. We never met, yet whenever we exchanged words over the phone his talks carried some profound effects unto my heart. I had first sent an email to Atreya asking on his postal address so that I could dispatch a review-copy of my book. He was so prompt in replying back, and shared his address with me. Atreya received the paperback on the eighth day of August, 2013. His text read as: "Received just now your cute book." On the following day I inquired whether he had read *The Unheard I*. In reply Atreya wrote: "I have fully read and enjoyed it, my article on your book will be published in the next issue of Muse India." The September issue carried the review, and I was awestruck! It was an extensive article on my small-volume nonfiction. As I rang him up to convey my thanks, he said, "It took two hours to fully read your book, Kiriti, but it took two days for writing the review." Atreya added, "I have had other commitments as well, trust me your book is truly engaging with so fewer pages in comparison with other titles, which are there on my desk right now." Destiny always plans in a different way, dear readers. I was taken aback as I received an email from Atreya much later, requesting for submission of my poems in *The Hans India*, a widely popular state-level English daily simultaneously published from Hyderabad, Visakhapatnam, Vijayawada, Warangal and Tirupati. It was one of my long poems that was published. I called up Atreya again to offer my gratitude, and he candidly replied, "You are finally there in Hyderabad *Hans*." Now, what would you possibly name this gesture? I never knew Atreya before, we never met in person, and I was blessed with his generous attempts towards showcasing my talent. Lately Atreya confessed, "I am not sure, but I always have had extremely good rapport with Bengalis, you know." The following poem is particularly dedicated to this benevolent human, worldly known as Atreya Sarma Uppaluri.

Clarity

I have seen my mother
preparing *Ghee* out of milk.
She never used butter to clarify
it any further!

My mother used to boil, and store
milk in large quantities for days;
upon cooling there was a thick
layer of screen, she separated
carefully. Layer after layer the screen
when filled the storage pot,
my mother put it on the burner slot.

I do miss the aroma nowadays.
The smell was so organic;
I do wonder why
we never termed milk aromatic!

Ah! Those granular residues that
took us to the heaven,
Ghee is pious, and incorrigible!

Rains

When I say "rains," I don't actually mean the shower that descends from the sky. Nor would I mean the plural form of the noun "rain." My "rains" denotes a situation, which makes me feel lost. I mean: Lost in the crowd, lost in my thoughts, lost in my occupation, lost in my discipline. These happen to everyone, I think, but they don't exert the same effect on the individuals concerned. Honestly, I have seen enough of "rains" for the last two years, and I am not in a position to afford anymore "rains." This has the wetting effect like the raindrops. But, my "rains" dampens the interior, and cannot be seen. Such intrinsic dampness consumes times to dry. In this chapter I will share a few poems that were written with my bleeding heart. Dear friends, my heart bled as it was punctured by "rains."

The Air

No one knew it was your
border vermillion that
made me kiss;
although stark,
it seemed a magical bliss.

No one knew it was your
iris brown that stored the
pupil blue;
they well call it my
instinct's hue.

No one knew I worshiped you
with my flaming heart;
no matter if I had a flower white,
you were to float, and fly
like the passing kite.

They say: "Love is in the air." This is a common saying, which, I think, is a high misnomer! I don't know who coined this saying first. Well, love is not a volatile thing, but a strong cerebral affair. We, the petty humans fall into the trap as soon as we consider love hearty. It is the brain, which governs the heart, and it is only the brain that makes us unaware of its crowning presence. Your heart can certainly nourish your brain, yet it is the latter that makes you the animal-best! Come on, this is not just about "you," or "I," this is just apt for all of "us." I have had my share of setbacks that originated from love, and yielded some scratches, which were only human!

Scratches Only Are Human

Few beautiful scratches, deep within,
soft marks, palpable even after months;
no wounds, but tiny scratches brown—
soothing, mesmerizing in between!

Lips uncut ... colored, covered are these
fine lines — sheer wonder.
Scratches see, smile, and talk

like palpating vessels, carrying
air straight into my balloons!

They smell divine, and growth enhancing—
climb the crown with shattered reflections,
moving fingers around, capture my
oozing spines...

I fell in love for so many times until now. Loving
someone is indeed a wonderful experience that
enables you to feel your loved-one inside you.
Falling in love is arresting indeed. I often wonder
about the agony that a failed motherhood suffers
due to the miscarriage or a stillbirth!
Motherhood is spontaneous, they say, and for
the men fatherhood is to be earned or acquired.
Even a man is prone to injury that affects his
nervous system. Men are no robots, which are
devoid of the mental stuff. The following poem,
I think, would elicit how I conceived love. Yes,
conception is the key word in the tune of love.

Stay Away

Feeling you wonderfully inside
never fails,
my nerves fail;
not again
not again

Feeling you beautifully inside
had been my dream;
questioning you straight:
Is there any more cream?

Feeling you humanly inside
is indeed a nightmare;
my heart sinks,
and I shrink sidewise...

Feeling you inside in
not again ... not again!

I am passionate about my shoes that I wear.
And I am particular too! Investing in a quality
pair is what I prefer rather than buying a cheap

pair of shoes. It is only my shoes, which I expect to be appreciated, for only they have witnessed my journey, and have absorbed all possible thrashings. During "rains" my shoes suffer from a no-use. I keep them in the dark, and they take absolute rest for days until I wear them again, and subject them to see the sun. Once I advised my son to write a creative essay on the topic: "If I lose my shoes." My son, Aishikk is now studying in grade three and enjoys creative writing. I told him, "Listen my boy, I will write a short poem on the same subject before you finish writing the essay." Aishikk, an eight-year old boy, was evidently confused. He came back to me and said, "I never lost my shoes before, and I really don't know what I will do if I lose them in future. All I can write is my mother will be angry if I lose my shoes. Please, give me some hints." I gave him a few points to elaborate. As he finished writing I told him to read my poem aloud. Although it was meant for the mature adults, Aishikk kept silent for some time as he read it. I realized lately that I did no good to my son by inviting him to read my poem on shoe-loss.

If I Lose My Shoes...

Did you make it rough?
I find it smoother but;
my skin has grown thicker, and
time has made its pleasant cut...

Paves turning their dustier best,
blacks and grays playing amidst—
rinses fall in its lap; poor I...
My soles crack finding the nest!

My "rains" continues to wet me even today. I
have now realized that only the lucky fellows
have experienced "rains" the way I felt. It is
inevitable, it is needed, and it keeps the human
alive in my wine!

Clips

My son dreams of fancy haircuts! My wife, Bhaswati and I are against his wish, for we nurture the notion that fancy haircuts suit the boys who are not serious in their academics. Friends, please, don't get us wrong. We have been brought up with the same theory that our parents used to employ. But, we have made it a point to get his haircut done from a professional salon that uses sterile clippers, and not the conventional age-old razors that do more harm than good. Clippers trim, and with expert hands they perform better than the scissors, which kill time to get the hair in shape as desired. Well, a clipper is used after parting the hair in segments by a few clips. Thus, clips play their roles in their significant, but small ways to the final look!

Most of my patients prefer to call it "clips," or "braces." They are not the ignorant types who are unaware of the actual name of the device that is used to correct the alignment of their teeth. These are the case-specific devices that we make out in order to position the teeth properly. We call it Orthodontic appliances, colloquially termed "clips." During my college days, I used to make collages of several photos and clips of my favorite film actress, and pinned those around my peripheral furniture. In fact, "clips" are the varied embracing entities, which tell their own story! Let us have a few literary [poetic] clips here:

In Tune

Remaining under self-control—
tongue and the heart have fallen in love;
look, zeroize them...

Be a bird!

Wide

On the ascending shoots
your fear matures,
as well as a few apprehensions new.
Your roots hold it tighter ... desperately
deeper
and much deeper rests your God...

Coming Home

I deck up my two ships
with the water that sky leaks

In the one I put
my gold, wealth, and all

The other has you, the deity,
and my childhood call.

Vermillion

My earphone whispers, and
lips glued to the chewing gum
my glasses moisten
as I find you eyesome
Is this what they call love?

In my childhood days I was surrounded by clips of words: clips of day-to-day events, exchanges of pleasantries, concerns, and many more. I like to refer letters too as "clips" of words. Letters clip us to varied entities. It may be an individual, an event, some emotional stuff, etc. I received my first clip from one of my school friends, Suprakash. We both were studying then in the fifth grade, and it was during our summer vacation when he sent along a postcard that bore his handwritten words. In reply I sent him my clips, asking about his whereabouts, and his wellbeing. This happened in the year 1984 that marked the assassination of our then Prime Minister, Indira Gandhi. Much later as my friend's father visited my clinic for a dental consultation he said, "Do you know I have carefully preserved the postcard that you sent to my son years back?" I was awfully surprised to realize that an elderly person had remarkably remembered my childhood "clips."

Creation

Would you mind a clue?

Small,
very small a hint...

Embracing the water
of the dawn ... ascent
and with falling down
the game turns decent!

The Odd Number

The night burns
with why, and whys.

Those inquiries in a row
end with the mark of sigh.

Scratches made by the nails, and teeth;
unknowingly biting
the lower lip,
and the nauseating smell that
spreads from the blanket damp.

Come on,
solitary in thy conjugal camp.

They call it a "lost art." Letter-writing, or as I have stated, "clips," are the ones that allow us to be creative with our words. It serves as a proven way to sketch our concealed psyche. With the advent of cell phones, emails, especially the World Wide Web, "clips" have taken a back seat. I think it is the basic poetic instinct that makes us write some wonderful short messages. Let us have a quick look here, and with these I end clipping you to my crazy pitch!

Vastu

The bedroom measures eleven by eleven,
twenty-two of you;
no mirror in the room
following *Vastu*.

A small family it is…

My Family

They are siblings;
the older fetches rain, while
the other burns my train

They keep on hugging
enticing my hunger and greed

My Master and the Cover

On the 31st day of October, 2013 Kunal Marathe [the publisher of the 1st edition of *My Glass Of Wine*] revealed the cover of my book on a social networking site. More than sixty guests wholeheartedly attended the virtual event. They were excited to see the cover of *My Glass Of Wine*, and greeted us with their honest remarks. Most of them were extremely eager to get this book in hand, but we received a few comments that posed a query: "What is the purpose of the vertical lines on the cover?" I asked my designer to say a few words on his design. Marut [the cover artist] said, "Look, you are a poet; if anyone asks you to explain your poetry would you do that?" I quickly replied,

"Not at all." Well, an art is to be interpreted by its followers, and not by the artist who has created the art. Honestly speaking, I found the cover enticing. Do you know why?

I initially planned to write on my spiritual association in the last chapter without which, I thought, my book would appear incomplete. It was only five minutes prior to the cover-reveal when I saw the design for the first time, and I was utterly surprised. I would like to let my readers know of the backlash: As my designer was commissioned I had to give him a brief of my book, plus I had to share my insights on the proposed cover design. Never in my wildest of dreams I imagined such a spiritually abstract design that would appeal to the general readers as well. Yes, in this chapter I will enlighten the cover through my Master.

Who is my Master? I have had numerous teachers who taught me the subjects. Right from the language, literature, science, mathematics, dentistry, etc., all were taught by my teachers. They have been professionally subjective to their approaches, and were considered brilliant.

They were the ones who made me score high in the examinations. But, when I say "my Master" I refer to the soul, who has graced my existence! The one, who allowed me to think, I am a human, and not just any other animal in this world — none other than my *Guru*, who is "my Master." My Master's approach is bloodless, mind-less, clueless, colorless, odorless, and noiseless! If I were to sum up His teachings in a few words, it would read as follows:

The Scripture

Open your heart, and
use your brain;
you will reach beyond
the humanly plane.

Act your actions,
mind His name;
God only dwells
within mortal frame!

My *Guru*, Dr. Ashoke Kumar Chatterjee is remembered as the World Kriyayoga Master, and he was conferred the title of *Yogacharya* [Master of Yoga] by His *Guru*, Sri Satya Charan Lahiree, the grandson of *Yogiraj Lahiree Mahasaya*. This is the basic history my readers must know before I write more on the interactions I have had with "my Master." It was in the month of March, 2008 I was initiated into Kriyayoga by Dr. Chatterjee. Until then I was not at all aware of the nuances of Yoga, and I was busy with the monotonous schedule of daily occupations. We all remain occupied, and so was I. My *Guru* first made me aware of my spine, and its invisible energy-centers. On the day of my initiation I was practically taught the principles of realizing the self. His divine wish allowed me to pen down the following poem:

Initiation

He made me sit on the square floor mat,
which I carried with my old bag.
I was not facing Him at first,

44

my centers were bare.
He first touched the base,
gradually coming up until
He held my cranial recess.
He directed me to face Him
with my eyes closed.
As soon as He spotted the third
the spirit echoed!
I fell in love with myself,
with the sole existence.

I wrote before: "My Master's approach is bloodless, mind-less, clueless, colorless, odorless, and noiseless!" Dear reader, let me please explain what I meant. Like other doctrines of worshipping God, we don't actually worship an abstract entity in Kriyayoga. Rather we worship the *Prana* [a Sanskrit word that means Soul] that keeps us alive. Kriyayoga is, thus, otherwise called *Pranakarma*. [*Prana* is Soul, and *Karma* is the action = action of the soul] The technique that is employed to worship the *Prana* is termed Kriyayoga. In this lineage an aspirant is allowed to live the life of a general householder. He/

45

she is not required to offer holy sacrifices in terms of killing the living animals and remembering God by drinking wine. However, the aspirant is able to taste the rich nectar wine that is believed to be secreted from the cerebral region. Kriyayoga allows one to reach beyond the mind. Lahiree Mahasaya once stated, "None is petty, it is the mind that is petty." [Ref: *Purana Purusha Yogiraj Sri Shama Churn Lahiree*, by Dr. Ashoke Kumar Chatterjee (Yogiraj Publications, Calcutta.)] As *The Bhagavad Gita* urges Kriyayoga is the supreme science, and is extremely confidential, hence clueless. Here a devotee is not allowed to disclose the process that is taught. There is no color code attached with Yoga. No red, no black, no saffron — one needs no colored attire to worship the soul. Again, an aspirant does not require burning incense and lighting candles to please the God! I think the most interesting feature of Kriyayoga rests in its quiet ambience. No loud prayers, no loud chanting are performed during the practice of self-realization. Thus, my Guru never altered my domestic existence, and blessed me with His sheer grace that made me write the following:

'I'

As identical as 'I'
through the slice of my sigh.
Like the sky;
where the stars shine bright and
the Sun 'I.'

Envisioning the Sun 'I' is said to be the primary motto of Kriyayoga. I have been graced by "my Master" far more than twice to realize my upright spine. Scripture suggests that the human spine consists of three fine channels or ducts, called *Nadi*. They are: *Ida*, *Pingala*, and *Sushumna*. Through austere practice of Kriyayoga the mother energy [called *Kundalini*] is awakened and She ascends through *Sushumna Nadi* that is located in between *Ida* and *Pingala*. This phenomenal transit of energy is often referred to as spiritual awakening or *Kundalini* awakening. Once it happens there is no looking back! The aspirant feels like living in a "winy trance."

Dear readers, please, have a look at the cover once again. It has two vertical lines and a glass filled with wine in between them. I suppose that the wine-filled glass represents the *Sushumna Nadi* that allows the serpentine She [*Kundalini*] to merge with the supreme He. I think that the vision of my cover-designer has aptly justified my untold plan of substantiating Yoga in the light of literature. I am not bothered if he agrees to my projection of his design, but again who is he to refuse my interpretation? I have interpreted his art in the light of Yoga, and some other may offer their thoughts on it. I believe here lies the success of an art-form, which has a generalized appeal, and some elements that make us think on it seriously!

Honestly, I am proud of being a follower of "my Master," Dr. Ashoke Kumar Chatterjee. He used to say, "Your mother is your first *Guru*, for she is the one who introduces your father to you." Whenever I remember these words I experience some ill-defined agony. Nowadays the global readers are much exposed to romantic novels, sexual thrillers, stories on murders, rapes, multiple relationships and betrayals. Our readers are the general public who are being offered attractive packages of open-ended relationships through novels and movies. Steady relationships are not considered so crucial these days. In terms of living a carefree life one has unknowingly accepted the status of a loner. Worldwide the psychologists are concerned about the increase in suicidal attempts by the students. There has been a surprising growth of adolescent crimes as well. We, in general, now have a lower level of patience, and we are intolerant of failures. We deliberately avoid self-analysis: Where am I heading to? I think that a generalized loss of faith in our ancient scriptures along with the sky-hitting urges of metropolitan lives have their shares of adverse effects, which are often covered by the worldly achievements. I am proud that I have "my Master," who supports me to unveil the mysteries of life. Let me conclude with the following poem:

Unravel

The rear desks are cleaner,
and the thriving crowd
enjoys fast food, lawsuits...

Healers worry about the front;
it is dusty, empty, but advocates
spiritual pursuits

My master enjoys the stage;
looking at the sparkling crowd he tells:
"Reach the void, and see the cage."

trespassers won't be prosecuted...
this is all about you and me!

The Reverse Tree

With all my heart I dedicate
The Reverse Tree
to the one who is an editor, a blogger, a
bestselling author, and above all a benevolent
human — my beloved friend
Donald Randolph Martin

You have numerous folders in your life since your birth until the last light. In all such folders you are given poetry in its nascent form. The moment one identifies and recognizes its spectacular lines they turn a poet!

my tree is stout,
well-developed
it refutes the gravitational pull

not always, you know...

my roots run
against the sap!

Anti-Clock

Men play their pivotal roles in reproduction, but do they produce? I highly doubt it! Men are not physiologically enabled to bear the fruits of production, and thus they are the non-yielding entities. Men are often referred to as trees, especially in familial setups, but none has specified yet if they are the male trees, which don't bear the fruits of love. If I ask you, what comes to your mind immediately as you think of a tree? I'm sure that your reply will include all or any of the following: a) flowers, b) fruits, c) green, or d) shade. Men are expected to be masculine, hence non-flowery. They are seedy, but are not eligible to carry the fruits. The signs of aging surface earlier in ladies, and men are ever-green. This is perhaps the only saving grace, for the ladies, all across the globe, who have proved their mettle as adequate 'servers' in their families. With service evolves dependence, and honestly, it is the ladies who turn out to provide better shade than the men. As you read these lines, would you still like to consider men as trees? Dear readers, I'm not here to change your mind, but I'm here to explain the salient features of *The Reverse Tree*; men are my keys!

In Others' Shoes

I'm sure, you must have mimicked someone at some point of your life. Mimicry is an art, if practiced wisely, which can entertain others and uplift the mood of your acquaintances. Not at the cost of injuring anyone's sentiments or disabilities, but mimicry is fun and it allows you to showcase your performer spirit. I'll tell you a story of one of my younger friends, Shouvanik Dey Banerjee, who is indeed great in getting into the soul of the person he makes his subject.

You are perhaps aware of Youtube, aren't you? And they host a wide range of cooking classes where the audience can learn the recipes of some delicious cuisines. It was a rainy morning as Shouvanik came to see me and inquired, "What will you cook for our lunch today?" I was happy seeing him after a long time, and I said, "Hey! Let me cook a chicken-dish that I have learned very recently." He was curious, "Where did you learn the recipe from?" I took out a small book from my cupboard and gave it to him, "This is the one I bought from the book fair this year. You know, it has some wonderful and quick recipes that are simple, and easy to follow."

Shouvanik went blank for some time; I could well understand that he was not happy with my answer as he asked, "You are such a net-savvy guy, and you are buying books to cook foods? This is ridiculous, why don't you surf through the Youtube recipes?" "Oh! I have never thought of surfing Youtube to learn a recipe, brother," I replied. Shouvanik kept mum for some time and approached my writing desk that had my laptop on it. My lappy had been kept on, and he quickly typed the URL: www.youtube.com. I guess it was my luck that the server was down that time, otherwise I would have missed a wonderful performance by my younger friend, and I could never get to know a mimicry artiste par excellence!

Describing his performance will be difficult, for the languages of one's gestures hate translation! However, I will give it a try. Shouvanik set out to teach me to prepare *laccha parantha* [a pancake that is a perfect accompaniment to the Indian non-vegetarian cuisines]. *Laccha* is spiral in form and is made of flour. My friend went on uninterrupted with his unique skill of mimicking the procedure as it was shown on Youtube. He mimicked a lady first, slightly changing his voice to a feminine tone, and explained the ingredients needed for the preparation. His fingers, wrists, and shoulders were in perfect synchronicity, and suddenly Shouvanik stopped for a while. He stood as he was just a second before. He was silent. I was surprised, and asked, "Hey! What happened?" He explained, "Haven't you experienced buffering while surfing Youtube?" I laughed out loud indeed, and he resumed thereafter. After every few minutes he made me see the Youtube buffering, and on every such occasion Shouvanik enlivened the session until he had finished with his teaching.

Yes, I did learn the recipe on Youtube even when my Internet server was down! It was Shouvanik who turned out to be an exact replica of a Youtube session as we'd usually see it online. It was his meticulous effort that entertained me ceaselessly.

Shouvanik spent a few hours in my home, we had lunch together, and in the evening he went on his way. I had a lingering thought. What was so hilarious about his mimicry? Why did I laugh at all? Hadn't this been difficult for him to get into the soul of a lady, as well as into the experiences of the Youtube viewers? His performance was funny, animated, and above all his sense of timing was just perfect! I think this is applicable to all genuine actors we see on screen, especially the comedians.

The question remains: How does one get into another being so effortlessly?

Long ... A Metaphor

Please spend a little more from your wallet, and ask your stylist if the wig you intend to buy resembles the texture and style of your lost hair. If you aren't careful, your audience will soon locate your fake affair with the hair. Well, I won't mind if you call me hairy! Hey, wait! I have a dangerously receding hair-line with marked male-type baldness! Being hairy is but being risky ... being difficult, or tough! As I wrote these lines I visualized a poet with long hair that was kept tied by an elastic band! Please read the following poem and ask yourself if this is only about creative writing:

a man dressed soberly…

almost like me
I know assessing brands
tactfully

a small earring on his right lobule
sorry, earring sounds
girly
I'll say a stud rather
with a rare white diamond in its center
you know, I can identify diamonds
as I'm trained
professionally

almost like me
a man dressed soberly…

I was then looking at his long hair
tied up at his back
his hair was kempt
I understood
readily…

people often accuse me of being poky
I go and meet men with long hair
unhesitatingly…

it was no exception today
I approached him
with a smile on my face
I was about to speak…
he said
I have failed to become a poet
miserably…

he moved away
he didn't wait for anyone
and I kept looking at his long hair
uninterruptedly…

I was sure
the man didn't notice my hair
intentionally…

The long haired male poets are generally taken
for granted. But why do they wear long hair? Is
it merely a matter of personal preference? Is
this in any way connected with poetry or art? In

India we used to have a hair-cleanser bar named "Crowning Glory" that was once endorsed by the well-known actress Dimple Kapadia. No wonder that worldwide a few of our male poets love to sport a feminine metaphor.

Crisis

I have been an ardent fan of poet Sumita Nandy's works. She is subtle, yet she is strong, and she writes sensuous Bengali poetry. It was with her *Desirous Water* [that I translated from its Bengali original, *Ichemoti*] where I could easily sense that she used a male voice in some portions of her poetry. She even confessed that in *Ichemoti* she wrote like a male, although I have found a mix of both the sexes in the book. Is this what we refer to as a third sex or gender? Here is a poem that I wrote as I read Sumita's *Desirous Water*.

I have matched my lips
with the highs of your water
as you flowed joy
the sun has dared to surface
on your mirror playing both
a she, and a he toy

I've my own equation of love
my he throbs in fire
while my she is coy

my girl shivers at times
she is frank, but shy
she hugs me in deep passion
wetting me with her thin soy

I worship the sun
powered by the rays
my she gives her all
as my he turns gay

I had once posted this poem on a social
networking site, and I got a quick message from
one of my friends in the United States, Linda

Bonney Olin. Linda is a God-centered poet, and she enjoys writing about Jesus, and especially Christianity. She was a bit hesitant in sharing her remark as she thought I would be angry at her input. Well, I'm game as far as my poems are concerned. Linda told me, "Kiriti, in the United States 'gay' is commonly used for homosexual men rather than its literary usage that means brightly happy." I was quite aware of this usage of 'gay,' but I had been experimental when I used that word in my poem. However, I sought advice from my editor Don Martin, who wrote a nice foreword for *Desirous Water*. Don, without even wasting a moment, opined, "Your readers of this book will understand the meaning of gay, so you need not change it." Quite evidently, my editor has reinstated my belief that readers are wiser than their authors!

Ah! I admit that the poem I cited above has a blend of both the sexes in a single frame, and although a poem is essentially omni-gender, I won't mind if my readers mark this poem 'bisexual.' But what is wrong in being gay? I'm

71

sure something is very wrong with the word 'gay.' My readers from the developed countries like the United States, United Kingdom, etc. may find it humiliating that in my country gay-sex is illegal and is a punishable offense! Gay men often refrain from expressing their sexual orientation in public and our society does not quite encourage a man who has a natural attraction to other men.

In our ancient *Vedic* literature sex is clearly divided into three distinct categories, *Purush* or male, *Stree* or female, and *Tritiya Prakriti* or the third sex. Gay men, lesbians, transgenders and transsexuals are considered among the third sex. India being the spiritual kingdom of the world, is dangerously defying the scriptural implications, as gay sex has been banned by the Supreme Court of India. While surfing through an article on a website [www. Mightylaws.in] about the representation of homosexuals [LGBT] in Indian literature, media and cinema I came across a unique representation that said, "The example of mixing black and white paint can be used, wherein the resulting color, gray, in all its many shades, can no longer considered either black or white although it is simply a combination of both." I strongly object to such a statement that represents homosexuals as gray, even if it was stated to clarify matters. If I take this statement for granted, I'm admitting the males as white and the females as black or the other way round. I think, none is black or white when it comes to representing sexual orientation or biasness. We all are biased in one way or the other in our day to day living, and who is the one that will paint us in any possible color? Colors mark racial discrimination.

In India like alternative medicine we have alternative literature that includes both *Dalit* literature and literary stuff that represents the third sex. I will be happy if the officials from the academic fraternity offer me the tag of an 'alternative poet.'

as my eyes open wide
I find myself sleeping with half-closed sight
you have come, isn't this right?

you know, I didn't sleep well

for many nights … many nights

I could hold you
while no candles lit
only my oil and the vermillion thread
were among the burning kit

you entered deep into me as did sleep

the moon shined bright
in your seminal light
for many nights … for many nights

A few years back as I wrote this poem I gave it to one of the widely published poets, Ranadeb Dasgupta, and he remarked, "A man searching his time in the tide of the eternal flow of human race." Under section 377 of the Indian Legislative Code gay sex is a punishable offence that may extend up to life imprisonment. I wonder how such a law can possibly exist in the world's largest democracy! Now another question is if India is truly a democratic country. However, I strongly believe sexual acts between two consenting adults [irrespective of their genders] can never be termed crime.

Let me share a true incident that I witnessed recently. Dear readers, owing to my professional employment I'm often located far from my hometown as well as my family, and I have to spend weeks in hotels that are located nearby my office. Well, you might be wondering why I stay in hotels, for there are other options to staying alone. A hotel is not that expensive a way of obtaining quality accommodations and good food, especially in the surroundings of my professional workplace. On the contrary, hotels are comparatively cheaper than the government allocated housing. Whatever, during my recent stay in one of those hotels I came across a man who was named Lara! Yes, Lara is a twenty-two year old chap who has opted and undergone a breast augmentation surgery. She prefers to be considered transgender until she gets her penis replaced by a surgically created vagina. I know after reading these lines you will be curious to know how I have gathered this information.

I met Lara just a month ago in the hotel; she looked like a lady, decent, and sexy, but she spoke in a manly voice and this made me curious to know more of her. I could have never known her biological sex had I not been given a chance to examine her physically!

It was a midnight, sometime in July, 2014, and I was busy working on some literary project as I heard an intermittent sound as if somebody was knocking at my door. I felt disturbed in the first place, but I had to open the door as I needed to find out who was there on the other side. I was surprised to see Lara weeping uncontrollably, and looking pale. I inquired, "What happened to you?" Lara was suffering from some excruciating pain as I could well assume from her gait, and she murmured, "My right breast is aching like hell, please, help me." I allowed Lara to enter my room. I locked the door, and asked her a few routine questions like when the pain started, nature of pain [throbbing, burning, piercing, etc.], etc. Lara didn't utter a single word; she pulled up her sleeveless vest and said, "Look, my breast is bleeding along the line of the suture." I was shocked to see her breast was oozing blood, and looked blue. I asked, "How did you get such an injury?" Lara kept aloof for a while and answered, "I am a transgender sex-worker, I was born male, and my right breast holds a silicone implant. One of my clients has badly hurt my breast tonight, and it is now aching extremely." I urged, "If you don't mind, may I examine your suture-line?" Upon careful examination followed by some general inquiry it was revealed that it had only been two weeks since Lara underwent breast augmentation, and she was not supposed to indulge in any sexual activity according to the instructions of her consultant surgeon.

Gradually I came to know more of Lara. Every evening we used to have our cups of coffee together, and we often dined out. Lara became my friend, but not my sexual partner in any sense. She once urged, "Doctor, if you ever get a chance to write on sexuality make me one of your characters, and please, don't hide my name." Lara was indeed a sport, and a very enthusiastic lady who never was afraid of revealing her sexual orientation. Lara preferred men and she liked to make love with them. As she said, she badly needed a boyfriend whom she could trust and make her life partner. With every passing day I developed more interest in Lara and I found her more inhibition-less. I asked her once, "What do you look out for in men?"

Lara surprised me with her unique answer, "I search for fresh & odorless sweat!" Lara was adamant about marrying a man. I often wondered why one would marry a transgender! What pleasure can a man derive from making love with another man who is feminine? How can a person marry someone who can never satisfy his needs the way a female can? My friend Lara was able to read my mind and one day she narrated her story of transition. Before I write her story, dear readers, here is a prose-poem that will make her more accessible.

You will call it fetish, I guess … I need some cologne as I step out of my home … odor that is mine …

physical ... deceptive ... I hate that smell ... it tells
the story of my communion ... time ... devotion ...
even the tales of my pillows ... it infuses poetry in my
being ... poetry arrives every now & then ... this is
alluring ... disturbing ... oh! sweat ... my sweat ...
don't you surface ... I'll now buy some anti-perspirant
... I'm safe...

Lara was born to a widow mother, and she was her only child. Her mother had been a working woman since Lara's father passed away. During childhood Lara was surrounded by her female friends in her neighborhood, and she enjoyed their company. She used to study in a co-educational school and she only had a few friends, all of whom were female. Gradually she started feeling like a girl trapped in a male body. She kept long hair like her female friends, and behaved like them. She carefully nurtured her female side that outgrew her male being. As she aged Lara became a complete female except for her physical attributes.

It was when Lara was studying her Masters in English Literature that she met a man, a few years older than her, who first expressed his interest in being Lara's boyfriend. Lara fell in love with this guy, Sumit. Sumit belonged to an orthodox Hindu Brahmin family, and he was sort of an introverted kind of a person. Sumit never introduced Lara to his family, but promised that he would take Lara someday to his parents and that he would make plans for their marriage. Lara was quite happy with Sumit, and they went out during the weekends and enjoyed each other's company. What happened thereafter was pathetic, dear readers!

All of a sudden Sumit started avoiding Lara saying that he had been occupied with his work lately. Lara was not allowed to see Sumit in his home, as he hadn't introduced Lara to his parents yet. Moreover, Lara was not aware of his residential address. Days, weeks and even months passed by. Lara was in deep pain being detached from her boyfriend, and one day she received a message on her cell-phone. It read: "Sorry, Lara, I am getting married next week. My parents will never allow you as their daughter-in-law, and I can't defy my parents. Hope you understand. I think you will find a better man who will satisfy your needs. Good bye!"

Lara fell ill, she didn't leave her home for months. She quit her college and sacrificed her Masters. She was not only shocked, she felt extremely humiliated by Sumit. Lara took almost six months to come out of this situation and planned for breast augmentation so she could work as a sex-worker to earn an independent living. She moved out of her home permanently and took shelter in a distant hotel.

As you read these lines, I am sure you too [as I did] will like to raise a few questions like: Why did Lara choose to be a sex-worker instead of completing her studies? Why did Lara never try to come back to her normal life and find her life-partner? I don't know whether you will ever get answers from Lara or from any other transgender sex-workers, but I can always quote a line or two that I used to hear from Lara frequently: "Kiriti, I dream of a lovely family, a caring husband and kids. You are such a spiritually inclined person, do keep me in your prayers, man!"

Living as a transgender is not an easy task, to say the least. I have seen Lara managing the role of a female that she was not naturally bestowed with, but she was a free spirit and took up the challenge with full enthusiasm. Although I never supported her plan of receiving the breast implant, I do salute her guts and strength of living a life on one's own terms.

Jet Lag

Welcome aboard! Flight "Poetry" will take you soon to the land of sleep where the scientists and poets work hand-in-hand, exploring its patterns, beauty, charm and its appeal. Thanks for flying with *The Reverse Tree*. I've never been an insomniac, dear patrons, but I have turned one of late. Thanks to my writing spree that made a non-poet write poetry! And this has indeed been a definite sleep-buster. How about a poem on sleep? You may give this a try:

> living inside air free
> I wondered, and thus,
> I reached a man-sized mirror

I see none else but me…

I see sleep
sitting idle bothside
beneath my eyes
tired
exhausted
upset

like the defeated me
smeared with much injured pride…
at the end of some trivial fights

I can only think of me as I now see sleep
I'm sympathetic
I feel like hugging it and saying:
"try a little more
you have come a long way indeed
only a few steps, come on … and there's your
core…"

sleep won't speak now
it appears disturbed,
least bothered to speak with…

I called out, "sleep…"
it didn't respond
called out again, "can you hear me, sleep?"
repeated
but to no avail…

oh! sleep is looking at me finally
smiling
it is coming up
from its corners

sleep embraces me at last
we are now locked to each other

sleep is speaking ceaselessly
I can see it, but I can't hear anything
its lips are vibrating
moving up & down
I can't hear sleep

want to say something, sleep
I urged
I pleaded
what happened to me

85

nothing else herein
none else
vacant otherwise
but only two of us
in the room for one…

My nephew, Chirantan [my older sister's son] who is now a citizen of the United States visits us once a year, and whenever he flies down to India, both he and my sister suffer from an acute jet-lag, and they experience a reversal of their biological clock. India is ahead by more than eleven hours from the U.S. time zones, so my relatives often sleep for hours at a stretch as they reach their native home. In an earlier chapter I wrote, "Colors mark racial discrimination." Although jet-lag affects our sleep pattern, it is not necessarily associated with the differences in time zones. Jet-lag is also induced by the differences in attitude of the people who facilitate the transit from one country to another. The following poem, I guess, can

render a jet-lag, even if you are yet to fly
through the air:

>they said you were black
>they knew they were white
>they loved their eyes

>the immigration officers were curious
>I pulled my sleeve up to the elbow
>showing them the mark
>they grinned...

>and I said
>this has been the *Nelson Mandela* patch

Reversal ... Reverse All

A tree that stands upside down appears amusing, for a tree is usually upright where its roots run under the soil, while its branches thrive caressing the sunlight. Here we have a tree that grows in the reverse order, and understanding the scriptural verses is but necessary to comprehend the other features of *The Reverse Tree*. Scriptures do not denote a particular religion, but they have evolved to protect humanity and mankind. Blessed I am that I've been taught the nuances of the last scripture of *Sanatana Dharma* [otherwise known as Eternal Religion], from an early age of my life. *Srimad Bhagavad Geeta* is supposedly the last available scripture that has been interpreted

88

by many scholars, sages, and monks in their unique ways down the years, and this is perhaps the only scripture that has been followed by the people belonging to other religions, like the Christians, Muslims, Sikhs, Jews, etc. *Srimad Bhagavad Geeta* is commonly spelled as *The Geeta*, and it relates the conversation between Lord Krishna and his follower Arjuna, one of the *Pandava*s of *The Mahabharata*. It had been on the war-front of Kurukshetra where Arjuna got bewildered as to kill his own relatives, his dear ones; wherein his charioteer Shri Krishna advised him of certain philosophical traits that made Arjuna face the consequences of the battle. *The Geeta* was originally written in Sanskrit, and it was aimed towards the understanding of our basic objectives of life. Later it has been translated into other languages, and thus, it has been made available to a vast range of readers.

The Geeta is the most precious gift to our civilization that has been much endangered by the animal-instincts of humans. Reversal of such animal instincts deserves austerity, and it demands our strict adherence to the lessons as laid down in the chapters. *The Geeta* consists of eighteen chapters, and it is believed that there were six-hundred and ninety-nine verses in its original version. However, the present version bears more verses which are said to have been introduced and added later. Before I get into the verses and their implications let me share a poem that I wrote about *The Reverse Tree*.

numerous branches of the root
unite into two soft halves
some creases fine facing the sky
here the sun fails to light
the cloud fails to moisten
nature shelters the root
secures within an encapsulating tough skin

the shoot is long and thick
smoother skin palpating beneath.
no study of the plants, but of humans,
the words of mouth
call upon true reversal

The Reverse Tree is not aimed to explain the verses contained in *The Geeta*, but I'll rather pick up a few significant ones that are my favorites, and interpret them the way I see my society and literature. My readers are hopefully aware of the recent Israel-Gaza conflict that killed innumerable people. Humanity took a back-seat, as the UN Secretary General Ban Ki-moon described the incident as a "moral outrage and a criminal act." In Kurukshetra humanity, lawfulness, trustworthiness, and integrity were restored as the Pandavas defeated the Kurus. *The Geeta* sets out with the following verse:

dharma-ksetre kuru-ksetre samaveta yuyutsavah
mamakah pandavas caiva kimakurvata sanjaya

[*O Sanjay, what did my sons, and the sons of Pandu do after assembling at the holy land of Kurukshetra?*][Chapter I, verse 1]

Kurukshetra was not just any other war-front, it had been the ground of establishing law, thus the word '*dharma-ksetre*,' which meant the place of pilgrimage. Moreover, conquering the fear that aroused from the loss of the worldly

91

bondages had been instrumental towards spiritual liberation. The twenty-second verse of the second chapter of *The Geeta* is stunning indeed:

> *vasansi jeernani yatha vihaya*
> *navani grihnati naro parani*
> *tatha sarirani vihaya jeernany-*
> *anyani sanyati navani dehi*

[*As a person puts on new garments while giving up the older ones, similarly the soul accepts new worldly bodies, quitting the old and useless ones.*][Chapter II, verse 22]

Don't mind if my take on this verse may sound off track. One of my friends, Razdan, who is now working as a marriage counselor has grown tired of fixing issues that have lately been surfacing in a large number of households. Values of relationships, marriages, and commitments have seen a drastic downfall leading to many instances of divorce, legal separation, and matrimonial discord. Now if one finds this a soulful occurrence, I won't possibly object, for people tend to adhere to the scriptural messages only on their superficial level.

My readers who are aware of my translation works often ask me how I manage the role of a translator. Translating a poem or a literary piece into another language requires much labor and sweat on the part of a translator. I would like to refer translation to as a transition as I allow the soul of the original poet to enter into my being. I am sure all successful translators will agree with my point that while translating literature the translator loses his/her own identity and receives the vernacular and language of the original poet. This is like suppressing one's soul for some time, while allowing another soul to ply within the conscious existence. Needless to say, the whole process is indeed exhaustive and painful at times.

I have often wondered how the soul of the original poem gets transferred to the translated version, and if the soul can be replaced voluntarily at all. If I suppose that if the first half of the previous line is right, it implies that after translating a poem/text of the original dies, but this is not the case under any circumstances. On the other hand, no translator can ever transfer the soul from its original location to its new destination as that is but the translated piece. A soul is an indivisible entity as *The Geeta* urges:

nainam chindanti sastrani nainam dahati pawakah
na caiman kledyan tyapo na shosyati marutah

[*The soul can never be cut into pieces by any weapon, nor can it be burned by fire, nor moistened by water, nor withered by the wind.*][Chapter II, verse 23]

An efficient translator constructs a faithful mirror that reflects the soul of the original literature. The more the surface area of reflecting body, the better is the image formed. But here the readers must possess the eyes that will allow the reflection to pass through their lenses and hit their retina. Having said that, a retina is not the biological retina that we usually talk about, but it is the sensibility of the readers who can smell, see and taste the original piece of literature through the image that is spontaneously formed by the translated work. Such eyes are rarely god-gifted; they have to be nurtured carefully through extensive studies of translated literature.

Enough though I wrote the word 'soul,' you may be wondering why your author has yet to explain his stand about it. Hey, wait! Read this poem and I'm sure you will understand what exactly I mean whenever I write the word 'soul.'

defining soul is difficult,
rather impossible
I have no doubt
I can perceive the 'I' in every decibel

my take is simple
it attracts dust
that smears the steps to the body temple

I press two fingers firm on my ears, and thus,
let the light dazzle my imprisoned candle

I walk early morning, wrapped in fresh silk

air entices, my skin shivers — I hear sounds
of click

in all works imperishable I listen to the
unheard...
bundles of joy, drops of eyes
make the 'I' a bard

I am aware of a few important literary journals that have made their stand very clear about the types of poetry they accept from their contributors. They are strictly against accepting a poem that has many 'I's' in it. Even the poetry-editors are afraid of the 'I' of the poet. Why is this so? I can only guess, but I'm not sure if I have the right answer. The modern breed of the poets and editors are not well-conversant with the scriptures of their respective societies. We can ask a Christian poet if they have studied *The Bible*. We can always inquire from a Hindu poet whether they have explored the mysticism of *The Vedas*, *The Geeta*, etc. And a Muslim poet can be asked about their relation with *The Quran*. My dear readers, studying or exploring the scriptures does not necessarily reflect a poet's belief in God or the Almighty. Even an atheist can read and research the religious texts and verses and enjoy the mystery of the words they are made of.

Let us take a quick look at a few verses from *The Geeta*:

tadviddhi pranipatena pariprasnena sevaya
updeksyanti te jnanam jnaninas tattva darsinah

[*Try to learn the truth from an Enlightened Master/ Teacher. Inquire from him submissively and render service unto him. Only an Enlightened Master can impart knowledge unto you because he has known the truth.*][Chapter IV, verse 34]

shradhavan-labhate jnanam tatparah
samyatendriyah
jnanam labdhva param santim acirenadhigacchati

[*One who is respectful to his/ her teacher can only acquire true wisdom, and can control the sensory organs. It is important that one cleanses their heart before approaching the Master, and once true knowledge is received liberation occurs in no time.*] [Chapter IV, verse 39]

The Geeta is not merely a collection of esoteric verses. Rather it is a time-tested literary-tool that can be employed towards self-development. This is perhaps one of the reasons that *The Geeta* is being taught in some of the best Business-schools in India and in other countries. One who teaches is a teacher — this has been a general definition, but when we say Master we mean something more. A Master is essentially a teacher, who teaches the truths of your existence! A Master guides you through the forest of life, so in every crucial juncture you have the courage and wisdom to face the inevitable challenges of life. Just look at the present-day scenario: People across all sects of life are impatient, restless, and refuse to pay respect to their seniors and elders. One may blame the evolving media & Internet culture, but this can never be the only factor that prevents people from offering respect to others. You give respect and you get respect. If this can be made a rule of thumb for every individual, life may turn out in a better way than it usually does.

I'll tell you my story. I have so many teachers in my life. I had some teachers in my school, a few more in my college, and moreover, I have a self-realized Master whom I refer to as *Gurudeva*. However, if I am asked to pick a single teacher who has shaped me and my life, I'll mention my mother. My mother used to be a high-school teacher who taught Economics to her students. Since my childhood she has not only inspired and motivated me, but she has also taught me in her own way that continues even now! My mom is a lady with indomitable spirit, and she hates to give up until she addresses the challenges to the best of her ability. Although my father had been a long-time religious devout, my mom never felt like visiting temples, offering prayers, or performing religious events in her home. However, she did all these with utmost perfection, as my father believed in them, and my mom never refused my father's words. Once my mother told me, "I have served my God through my service to your father, you, your sister, and through my duties towards my family." I've often taken my mom for granted; this was not to hurt her, but just as another grown-up man who refuses to accept his mother's words under the impression that his mom is now dated!

The eleventh day of May is celebrated as Mothers' Day in India, and this year I gifted her a poem that I wrote exclusively for my mother.

you were evaluating the answer-scripts
I was thrilled...
this was the way I picked up
the nuances of your major, Economics

do you remember
it had been years back
I was in my seventh grade
down with high fever

I was about to fetch, perhaps
a glass of water...

I don't remember what happened next...

I opened my eyes only to find
myself in your lap
you were sprinkling water on my face

tapping mildly my forehead

"what did you see, my son?" you questioned
my response was firm and audible

"Ma, I saw *Lord Rama* and his divine spell."

Coming back to another verse of *The Geeta*. In chapter XV, verse 1 God has first explained the implications of *The Reverse Tree*:

urdhva-mulam adhahò-sakham
asvattham prahur avyayam
chandam si yasya parnòani
yas tam veda sa veda-vit

[*There is an imperishable banyan tree that has its roots upward and its branches down and whose leaves are the Vedic hymns. One who knows this tree is the knower of The Vedas.*][Chapter: XV, verse 1]

Humans are the only such trees that have their roots [brain] up and the branches (limbs) down. The whole concept may appear abstruse for one who hasn't yet studied spiritual texts, but *The Reverse Tree* has no intention whatsoever to bring you close to God or godly messages.

Removing agony from life is not an easy task unless we recognize the source. This is all about the worldly attachments that we grow knowingly or unknowingly, and at times such attachments outgrow our search for truth. Agony surfaces right there. I did a small experiment with a few poets and writers recently. I told all of them to write an epitaph that would be published in an anthology. I named the anthology *Epitaphs* and I approached one of my previous publishers who readily accepted my proposal. I got flooded with queries from contributing poets and writers. Most of them asked: "Whom will the epitaph be written for?" I simply responded, "As you think right." We received more than one-hundred and fifty submissions from across the world, and surprisingly only a few wrote epitaphs about themselves.

Although an epitaph is essentially a Western concept, our poets and writers, irrespective of their cast, creed and religion accepted and participated in this anthology wholeheartedly. Most of them wrote for their departed family members, and dear ones. My concern is: If the poets fail to consider death as an inevitable reality, what will be the readers' stand? I wrote a short foreword for *Epitaphs* and my concluding line was, "Enjoy life even in death!"

Reversal happens indeed! It is not like the anti-aging crème that you may find in the beauty-salons, but reversal demands practice of the principles that lead us towards truth or realization. Human-birth is graced as one understands the challenges of life and implements wisdom to stand up to them. *The Reverse Tree* is all about our understanding of the existence of mankind…

I'm no linguist…

I know
air and age are linked
since eternity…

and the wounds surface again
in all directions…
sporting the guise of youth…

Healing Waters Floating Lamps

To the great poet ... the legendary ... the
unputdownable...

Rabindranath Tagore

On the ascending shoots
Your fear matures
A few apprehensions as well
Your roots hold it tighter
Desperately deeper

And much deeper rests your God

Beyond The Eyes

I reach the sky
While I draw a circle in the water

Looking at the image

I take a dip

After Bath

I've bathed your feet with the water of the
Ganges
Last dip in the late afternoon, and
I paid my first obeisance
While my body was smeared by the earthen mud

I walked down the broken stairs
With a stony heart
One step down, and down again

I cannot learn swimming ... scared even now

I would not offer a homage anymore
As I offered prayers for the last time

O Sun, I remember
I've bathed your feet with the water of the
Ganges...

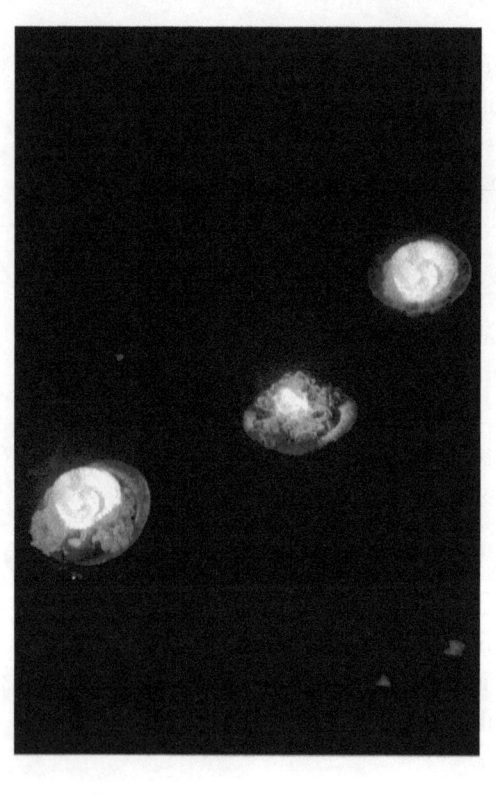

Evening Varanasi

Have you seen the floating lamps in the river?

Water here is not the fire-extinguisher, but
The flames ascend through water

Prayers reach the meditating Lord

River Of Tears

They have flowed over your eyes
Afraid of being seen
They are shy

In spite of their roomy eyes
They are blind

They don't know
Not all rivers succeed to unite

Unravel

The rear desks are cleaner
And the thriving crowd
Enjoys fast food, lawsuits

Healers worry about the front;
It is dusty, empty, but advocates
Spiritual pursuits

My Master enjoys the stage—
Looking at the sparkling crowd he tells:
"Reach the void, and see the cage!"

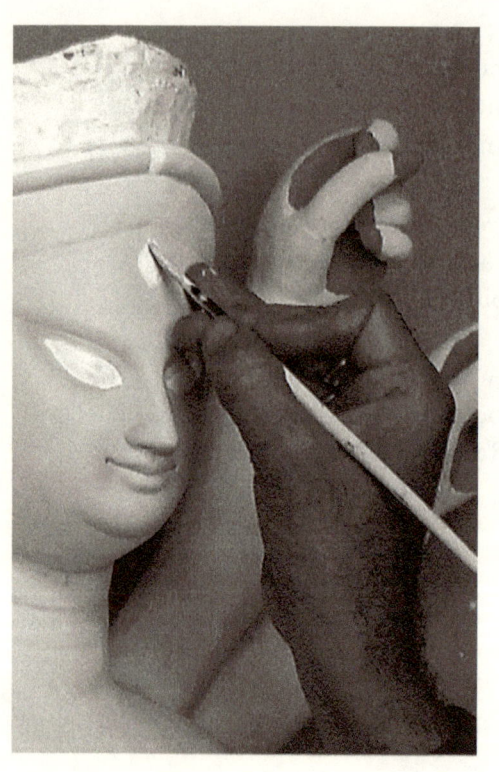

Initiation

My Master made me sit
On the square floor mat, which was brought
In the old bag
I was not facing him at first
My centers were bare
He first touched my base
Gradually coming up
Until he held the cranial recess

He directed me to face him
With my eyes closed
And as soon as he spotted the third eye
My spirit echoed

I fell in love with myself
With the sole existence.

In Dusty Feet

I was about to prostrate,
But refrained from paying an obeisance
To the enlightened Master
His great toes housed
Some holy grains of dust
He took good care of his feet, I guessed,
And I picked the grains as quickly
As to place them on my head

I followed his footsteps,
Even on the dusty roads
I wished to become such pious grains
So as to stay attached with his feet forever

I turned back as I failed,
And could not hold the grains either
On my big toes…

God remained thumb-sized with dusty feet

Eyes Of A Yogi

A mother bird sits on her eggs … quiet…
Her eyes appear distantly connected to the world

Hey! Look at them
Tiny wings

The mother changes to sky

Communion

The woman in you is sleeping for eons

She wakes up, and
Traverses a lane named serpentine

The Enlightened Master

Your teeth never show
As you smile
The world thinks you're tight lipped

You've been flooded with appeals,
And advice to see a speech-therapist,
Or a dentist

Please say, we pleaded…

Did we forget a Yogi seldom breathes?

Color Code

They said you were black
They knew they were white
They loved their eyes

The immigration officers were curious
I pulled my sleeve up to the elbow
Showing them the identifying mark
They grinned...

And I said
This has been the *Nelson Mandela* patch

Clarity

I have seen my mother
Preparing *Ghee* out of milk—
She never used butter
To clarify it further

She'd boil and store the milk
In large quantities for days
Once cooled, she'd separate
Thick layers of yellow froth—
Layer after layer she filled
The storage pot, then put it on
The burner, which filled
The house with aromatic milk

So organic is my memory—
The granular residue lifted us to heaven
Ah! Pious *Ghee*, and incorrigible

Indian Matrimony

After your sister's wedding her in-laws never failed to pass their comments: "Water and oil don't blend at all…" You could not answer them; they were the respectable elders. You found your sister sweating … her skin became pale and cold.

You went ahead and explained to them the relationship of economic inflation and the price of crude oil.

You concluded: "Water leaves no mark behind as it evaporates…"

Not in water,
But awake
In the soil

Some poison
Blue…

The venom doesn't fade

Doesn't float
And doesn't even invite!

Touching only a few fingers...

Namesake

1.
Whispers the tale of your character
Color and its fragrance merge to call it a rose
A lot matters
If you remember the name…

2.
With sheer innocence the boy told the story of his watching movies in a hall named *Nadia Talkies*. Sharing the same story for many a time, uttered the name, talkies, and had his face shine! Humble was the hall, so were its viewers. Alas! It is no more … abolished by the estate promoters! The boy is now a grown up man … Nadia remains inside its reel-can.

3.
The womb carries water — so do your eyes
Water builds the fetus
That becomes 'I'
It's a room for the eyes—
Under the name: 'Rely'

4.
Significant indeed — carrying yourself
Crucifixion is Christ-filled!
I remember, and my mind turns candle-lit

They pinned it before,
Will do that now and again…
No arrangements of incense though

God and life
Moving apart

Mellifluous Cry

The labor room was busy as usual
Especially the midwife
She was visibly unhappy with the silence of the
newborn
Much worried at it, she patted the back of the
baby

The midwife screamed in utter frustration
"Hey! Cry out."

On the other side of the closed door
The father was eager to hear his baby

He was all set to smile and celebrate
The first communication

Secure A River

Hold on, my dear
The word "denser" does not
Necessarily mean thicker
Divine blessings are frequently showered
Unconditionally
The enlightened Masters across the nations
Prefer to name the phenomenon
"Without-A-Cause"
I saw you smiling at your fat donation

Your ailing parents needed you badly
Expecting your assuring presence
You had been calling the payment desk
Every now and then
Only to confirm they had their insurance
Alive

Your parents informed the nurse
A spoonful of water was all they wished
But they departed without you at their bedside

The doctor said your parents didn't struggle
They never complained of your absence
Happy with their pills
They handed over their last will

A piece of paper ... a few words written on it
"When you have time, my child,
Come to the river..."

Memorandum Of Understanding

I'm no linguist!

I know
Air and age are linked
Since eternity

And the wounds surface again
In all directions
Sporting the guise of youth…

Sleep ... Yet To Arrive

As my eyes open wide
I find myself sleeping with half-closed sight
You have come, isn't this right?

You know, I didn't sleep well
For many nights ... many nights

I could hold you
While no candles lit
Only my oil and the vermillion thread
Were among the burning kit

You entered deep into me as did sleep

The moon shone bright
In your seminal light
For many nights ... for many nights

Celluloid

Gold is precious and so is the time
We spent together ... right from the morning
tea
Spanning over the lavish lunch until you said,
"Signing off for today."

I was hesitant, you know,
I never said goodbye

Signs are private, and I keep my eyes open
Round the clock

Fish-Lip

I've read morphology of the fish-lip
Gives hint of the water color deep

A small aquarium inside my living room …
cornered—
Marks of love and kisses
On either side
Even on its face

My lips are thin
No trace of color, but water…

Scratches Are Only Human

Few beautiful scratches, deep within,
Soft marks, palpable even after months—
No wounds, but tiny scratches brown
Soothing, mesmerizing in between!

Lips uncut ... colored, covered are these
Fine lines ... sheer wonder
Scratches see, smile, and talk
Like the palpating vessels that carry
Air straight into my balloons

They smile divine, and growth enhancing—
Climb the crown with shattered reflections,
Moving fingers around, capture my oozing
spine...

The Odd Number

The night burns
With why, and whys
Those inquiries in a row
End with the mark of a sigh

Scratches made by the nails
Unknowingly
Teeth bite the lower lip

Nauseating smell
Spreads from the damp blanket

Solitary in thy conjugal camp...

The Sun

This is not all about
Day-light photography

This is rather reaching you
As if you're the destination...

Close Circuit

Had not this been fragile
I would have positioned
A camera upon my collar-bone
On either side

And then
I would have removed the extra lenses
One by one…

Ah! Such impeccable folds of civilization

The Morgue

None has claimed the body yet ... it won't speak on its own ... to announce identity ... distended with an unborn life, it seems ... the cover falls short ... and the limbs remain exposed...

Those feet can't take them to the church ... fingers can no longer light candles...

Wish I could burn incense inside the dead room ... inviting lives ... turning the body into a temple...

Give Me More Of Life

Amusing, but real...

A young girl was standing
At the bank of a river
Her hands held a live *Koi*
I was curious, and she said,
"Hold it and you will understand."
She ran away flashing a quick smile

I surfed through the radio channels
On my cell-phone
I heard a commentary of The Gita
A speech on the Visvarupa Darshan

The cellphone blinked
I saw a message my friend sent
A famous line by Tagore—
"Chokher aaloy dekhechilem chokher bahire"
[I envisioned the external through the light of
my eyes]

Adios

The mirror has a limited role as we urge,
"Please, visit us again."

Immersion happens only in the water
People gather … they sing and dance
Only a few of them have their eyes moistened

Rituals of self-reflection end
With gods and goddesses
The river turns pregnant

Since Time Unknown

I have not reached yet
The science of you … I know
I'm glued to, and stand still
With some fixations
Since time unknown
You spin … continue to swivel
You have a firm grip

Faulty are my limbs
They tilt even on the steady floor
I readily realize
It is all in my mind
As the sky swings

You spin and continue to swirl
Since periods unknown

Notes

My Glass of Wine was first published in India [ISBN-13: 9788192861906, Paperback] by Author's Empire Publications Pvt. Ltd. [New Delhi] in December, 2013. The book was revamped and the expanded second edition [ISBN-13: 978-81-931666-8-0, Paperback] was released by Hawakal Publishers [Calcutta] in August, 2015. In both editions the cover was designed by Marut Kashyap.

The Reverse Tree was first published in India [ISBN-13: 978-93-84180-77-5, Hard Cover] by Moments Publication [Ahmedabad] in October, 2014. The cover was designed by Tamojit Bhattacharya.

Healing Waters Floating Lamps was first published in India [ISBN-13: 9789384180232, Paperback] by Moments Publication [Ahmedabad] in March, 2015. The cover was designed by Marut Kashyap.

Page **i**: Dr. Casey Dorman's commentary on the three books was first published in *The Statesman* in January, 2016.

Page **xi**: *Make Me Some Love to Eat* has been released in 2016 by i, write, imprint.

The dedication-page in *My Glass of Wine*: hülya yi lmaz is the Senior Lecturer of the College of the Liberal Arts, The Pennsylvania State University, U.S.A. She teaches German language and literature. She also teaches Comparative Literature and Turkish. She has authored *Trance*, a collection of her poems. yilmaz is also the author of a scholarly book, *Das Ghasel des islamischen Orients in der deutschen Dichtung*. Her most recent research has resulted in other publications, including a book chapter, "The Imagined Exile: Orhan Pamuk In His Novel Snow" in *Global Perspectives on Orhan Pamuk: Existentialism and Politics* (2012).

Page **17**: Nadia is one of the prominent districts of West Bengal, India. *Nadia Talkies* used to be a popular movie hall, an auditorium located in *Nabadwip*, a suburban town within the district, Nadia.

166

Page **26**: A swan is called *Hans* in India, and is believed to be the carrier-animal of *Devi Saraswati*, the goddess of wisdom.

Page **40**: *Vastu Shastra* [*vâstu* , also *vastu veda* and *vastuvidya*, science of construction, architecture] is an ancient doctrine which consists of precepts born out of a traditional view on how the laws of nature affect human dwellings. The Sanskrit word *Vastu* means a dwelling or house with a corresponding plot of land. Courtesy: Wikipedia

Page **113**: Water of the Ganges, otherwise called Ganga-water, is considered extremely pious, and is widely used in all Hindu religious affairs. And again, the Hindus offer homage to the Sun (called *Surya-pranam*), as it is the sole source of all energies.

Page **115**: Varanasi [otherwise known as Kashi] is considered the spiritual capital of India [and India being the spiritual capital of the world]. Lord *Shiva* is worshipped here with full devotion and in the evening the devotees place tiny lamps [*diya*s] in the river Ganges.

Page **127**: An individual carries both a he and a she-energy. The 'she' when awakened traverses the spiral *Kundalini* along the spine and merges with the 'he' that resides at the top of the cranium, commonly referred to as the *Sahasrara*. Upon successful communion an individual turns a Yogi!

Page **159**: *Koi* is a fish that survives for a few hours if kept out of water. In Bengali a girl's life is colloquially referred to as a *Koi*'s life, for they can withstand all the hazards that they face.

Acknowledgements

My parents are my primary teachers. I am grateful to my mother, Roma Sengupta, who first taught me the English language. It was her indomitable spirit that I got from her. My father, K. S. Sengupta is the one who always encouraged me to build my English vocabulary. During my early academic life he gifted me the voluminous Collins Cobuild advanced dictionary, which I keep on my bedside table even today.

I am thankful to my wife, Bhaswati, for allowing me the space that was needed to pamper my pen. I respect your sacrifices, my sweetheart!

I love you my son, Aishikk, for understanding the pain I bore during my staying away for wccks from you. I believe that a son understands his father the best!

I am thankful to the bestselling novelist and editor, Don Martin, for editing the three books prior to their publication.

I'm grateful to all reviewers and journals that have published the reviews of my books.

My friends: Bitan Chakraborty, Kaushik Acharya, Munshi Younus, Prabir Roy, Shouvanik Dey Banerjee and Vishal Joshi — my back-up support!

Photographs in *Healing Waters Floating Lamps* came from Arindam Chowdhury and Somnath Chatterjee. I'll love to thank them for allowing us to use their photographs.

Hawakal helped me to get set for the trilogy. I'm grateful to them.

Critical Acclaim for Kiriti Sengupta

[Sengupta's] work reads like an exploration of life — seen from the Yogi's angle — and an acceptance of its universality and uniqueness. We are taught that Yogis meditate to bring the Mother to the Father, a metaphorical journey that describes the climb of energy up the spine in meditation. Much of Sengupta's imagery stems from this symbolic process.

Lost Coast Review

With great simplicity [Sengupta] tackles issues of love, spirituality, relationships, the world and nature as he perceives them and brushes them with his poetic sensibility. He cracks open little drawers and lets us peek into some uplifting moments of his life. The poetic vision he lends to his experiences and deep meditation on things we take for granted in our indifferent stride, shakes up our mental lethargy and prods us to reflect intensely on such matters.

The Fox Chase Review

[Sengupta] is not soliloquizing; rather he creates an alter-ego of himself to speak to. A very common and routine view turns poetic through his voice, his expressions, and through his experiences.

Wilderness House Literary Review

www.kiritisengupta.com

Kiriti Sengupta is a poet, editor, and translator from Calcutta, India. He has published nine books of poetry and prose; two books of translation; and is the co-editor of five anthologies.

www.ingramcontent.com/pod-product-compliance
Lightning Source LLC
Chambersburg PA
CBHW020116180626
46812CB00006B/2618